Abby Visits the Big City

The City Mouse and the Country Mouse Remixed

BY CONNIE COLWELL MILLER   ILLUSTRATED BY VICTORIA ASSANELLI

AMICUS ILLUSTRATED is published by Amicus
P.O. Box 1329, Mankato, MN 56002
www.amicuspublishing.us

For Abby, the busiest bee, with love. —C.C.M.

LIBRARY OF CONGRESS CATALOGING-IN-PUBLICATION DATA
Names: Miller, Connie Colwell, 1976- author. | Assanelli, Victoria, 1984–
   illustrator. | Aesop.
Title: Abby visits the big city : the city mouse and the country mouse remixed / by Connie
Colwell Miller ; illustrated by Victoria Assanelli.
Other titles: City mouse and the country mouse remixed
Description: Mankato, MN : Amicus Illustrated, [2017] | Series: Aesop's fables remixed |
Summary: "In this modern-day re-telling of Aesop's fable 'The City Mouse and the Country
Mouse,' Liz turns up her nose at farm cooking while Abby learns she prefers the peace of the
farm to the excitement of the city" — Provided by publisher.
Identifiers: LCCN 2015034231 (print) | LCCN 2015051290 (ebook) | ISBN 9781607539520
(library binding) | ISBN 9781681510767 (ebook) | ISBN 9781681510767 (pdf)
Subjects: | CYAC: Fables. | Folklore.
Classification: LCC PZ8.2.M488 Ab 2017 (print) | LCC PZ8.2.M488 (ebook) | DDC
398.2—dc23
LC record available at http://lccn.loc.gov/2015034231

EDITOR: Rebecca Glaser
DESIGNER: Kathleen Petelinsek

Printed in the United States of America at Corporate Graphics in North Mankato, Minnesota.

10 9 8 7 6 5 4 3 2 1

ABOUT THE AUTHOR

Connie Colwell Miller is a writer, editor,
and instructor who lives in Mankato,
Minnesota, with her four children. She has
written more than 80 books for young
children. She also likes to tell stories to
her kids to teach them important life
lessons—just like Aesop did in his fables.

ABOUT THE ILLUSTRATOR

Victoria Assanelli was born during the
autumn of 1984 in Buenos Aires, Argentina.
She spent most of her childhood playing
with her grandparents, reading books, and
drawing doodles. She began working as
an illustrator in 2007, and has illustrated
several textbooks and storybooks since.

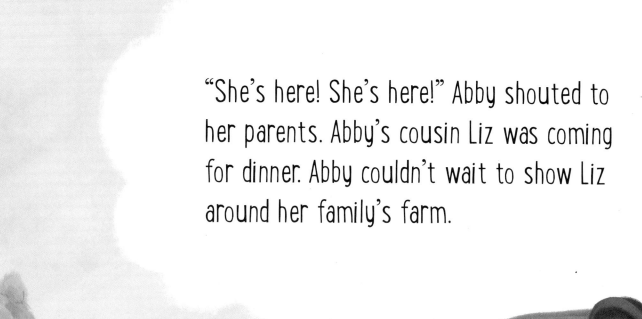

"She's here! She's here!" Abby shouted to her parents. Abby's cousin Liz was coming for dinner. Abby couldn't wait to show Liz around her family's farm.

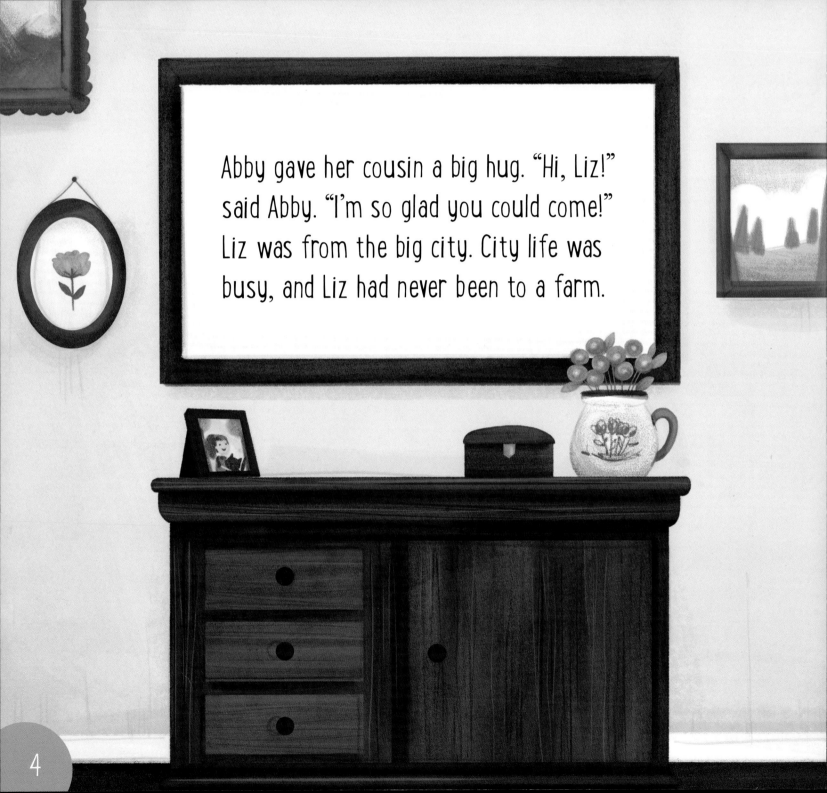

Abby gave her cousin a big hug. "Hi, Liz!" said Abby. "I'm so glad you could come!" Liz was from the big city. City life was busy, and Liz had never been to a farm.

"The baby pigs were just born," Abby told Liz. "I'll show you." Liz did not like the smell of the hog barn. Before long, Abby's mother called the girls for dinner.

Abby's mother dished up a plate for Liz. Liz looked at the food in surprise. "Is this the food you always eat, Abby?" Abby looked at her plate. It was pork chops, green beans, and a biscuit. Abby said, "Yes. This is my favorite meal!"

Liz said, "In the city, we have all kinds of food! Pizza, pasta, tacos, burritos—even sushi! It's much fancier than this food." Abby didn't know what to say. They didn't have those foods on the farm.

Liz went on. "You should come eat in the city tomorrow. You'll see." Abby enjoyed the food her parents served. But she did want to see the big city. Abby looked at her parents. "May I go?" she asked. Her parents nodded yes.

The next day, Abby went with Liz and Liz's parents to the city. The lights of the city were beautiful. They chose a fancy Italian restaurant for dinner. It was crowded. They waited for a long time.

Finally, they sat down and ordered their food. All around, people were talking and shouting. Pots and pans were banging. Abby was nervous. The food was tasty. But she felt rushed to get out of the busy restaurant.

After dinner, Liz and Abby walked to the car. They stepped off the curb together. Suddenly, a car zoomed by them, honking loudly. Both girls were forced backward. "That car almost hit us!" Abby shouted.

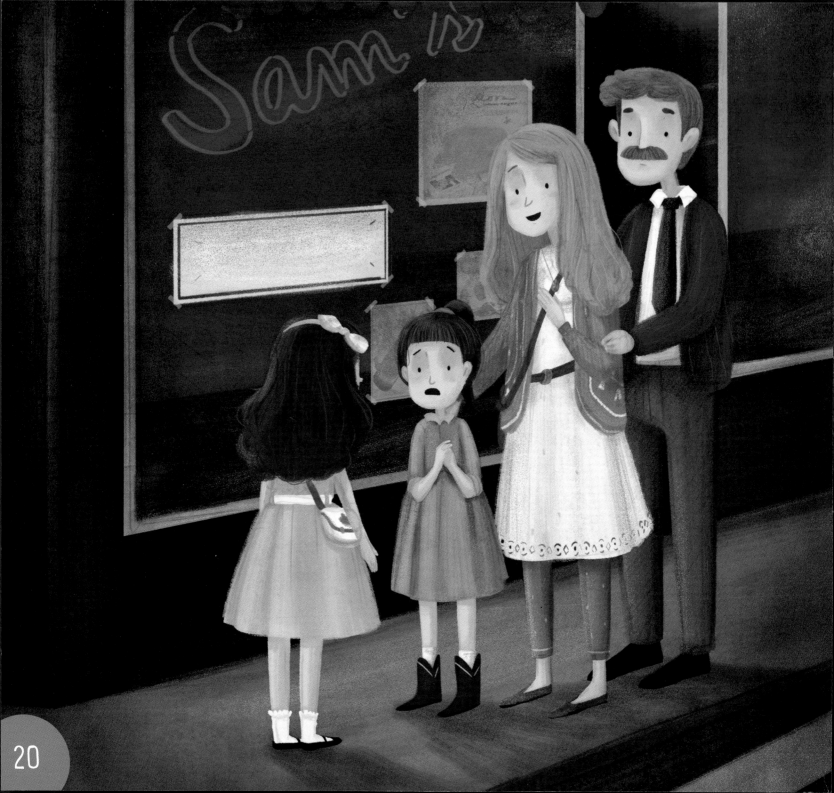

The girls were safe. But Abby was tired of the city and ready to go home. She looked at Liz. "Your food is fancier here. But I would rather eat simple food in peace and safety than eat fancy food and be in danger."

Liz looked surprised. Then she said, "I guess there are good things about both places."

The City Mouse and the Country Mouse

by Aesop

Once upon a time, a city mouse visited his cousin in the country. The mice had a simple, quiet meal. The city mouse told the country mouse that he had much more food in the city. So he invited his cousin to come with him to the city.

The country mouse agreed, and the next day they traveled to the city. The city mouse showed the country mouse all the wonderful scraps they could get in the big alleys of the city. However, as they were eating, a large cat approached. The mice had to scurry away and wait for the cat to leave.

The country mouse decided to return to the country. He told his cousin, "Yes, you do have more food in the city, but I would rather enjoy my dinner in peace."

Moral: A simple life with peace and quiet is better than a rich life with danger and fear.

23

Discussion Questions

1. How is Abby similar to the country mouse in the fable?

2. How is Liz similar to the city mouse?

3. What lesson does Abby learn?

4. What lesson does Liz learn?

5. Can you think of a time in your life when you have behaved like Abby?

6. Can you think of a time when you have behaved like Liz?

7. How is the story of Abby and Liz different from the original fable?

8. How are the two stories similar?

Who Was Aesop?

Many people believe that Aesop was a storyteller from Ancient Greece. He told stories about animal characters that did human things. Aesop's stories were spoken out loud. Later, other people gathered the stories in a collection that is now referred to as "Aesop's Fables." Each of Aesop's fables shares a moral, or important lesson, with the reader.